KU-299-363

How to Make
Christmas Tree Decorations

First published in Great Britain 1997 by
SEARCH PRESS LIMITED
Wellwood, North Farm Road, Tunbridge Wells, Kent TN2 3DR

Originally published in Germany by
FALKEN Verlag under the title *Weihnachtlicher Baumschmuck selbstgemacht*
Copyright © FALKEN Verlag 1996

English translation © Search Press Limited 1997

Cover design: Andreas Jacobsen
Editor: Heike Schulz
Production: Ulrich Klein
Photography: Carsten Cramer
Pattern design: Daniela Schneider

The Publishers would like to acknowledge the following authors for their
contributions:
Petra Boniberger for pages 8–11, 12–13 (String baubles), 14–17, 34–35
Regina Hipp for pages 20–23
Iris Kasperek for pages 40–51
Silke Koers for pages 24–25, 30–33, 36–37, 52–53
Monika Lüttecke for pages 26–27
Monika Neubacher-Fesser for pages 12–13 (Golden shapes)

ISBN 0 85532 831 2

All rights reserved. No part of this book, text, photographs or illustrations,
may be reproduced or transmitted in any form or by any means by print,
photoprint, microfilm, microfiche, photocopier, or in any way known or as
yet unknown, or stored in a retrieval system, without written permission
obtained beforehand from Search Press.

Readers are permitted to reproduce any of the items/patterns in this book
for their personal use, or for purposes of selling for charity, free of charge
and without the prior permission of the publishers. Any use of the models/
patterns for commercial purposes is not permitted without the prior
permission of the publishers.

Printed in Spain by Elkar S. Coop. Bilbao 48012

How to Make
Christmas Tree
Decorations

Petra Boniberger
Regina Hipp
Iris Kasperek
Silke Koers
Monika Lüttecke
Monika Neubacher-Fesser

SEARCH PRESS

Contents

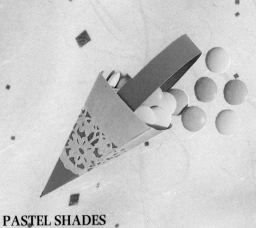

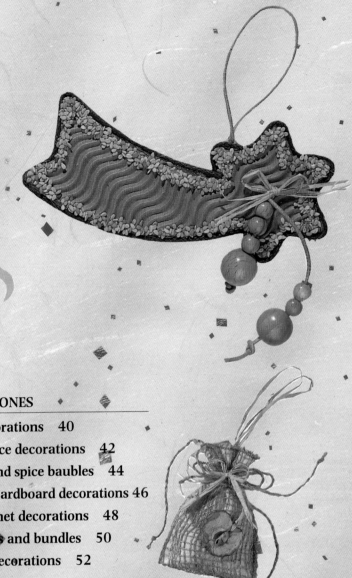

Golden Hues

The traditionally festive colour of gold always makes a Christmas tree look rich and luxurious. The following pages show how to create gleaming stars, bells, crowns and many other Christmas decorations – all of which make beautiful and practical alternatives to those which can be bought.

Angelic baubles

These baubles are made using a collage of angels cut from paper serviettes or wrapping paper.

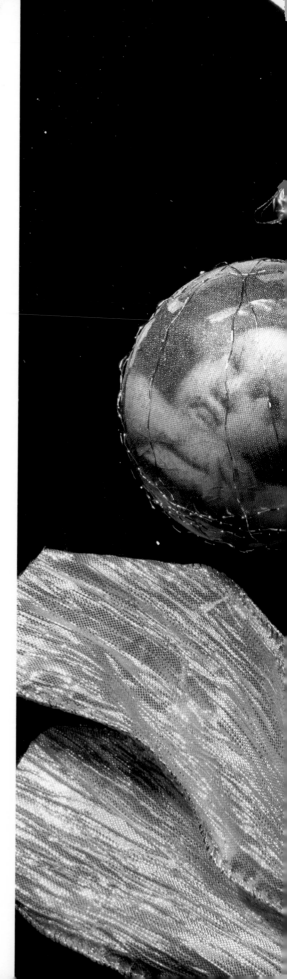

1. Cut out pictures of angels from paper serviettes or wrapping paper.

2. Mix up a small amount of wallpaper paste, following the instructions on the packet. Brush the wallpaper paste on to a polystyrene ball. Overlap the pictures of angels to cover the ball. When completely covered, brush the ball all over with a little paste and then leave to dry.

3. Insert a few pins randomly over the ball, leaving just the heads visible. Wind twists or spirals of fuse wire or fine copper wire around the pin heads until the ball is encircled with wire. Press the pins completely into the ball.

4. Paint small feathers with gold paint. When dry, weave them into the wire.

5. Thread gold beads on to pins and stick them into the ball to decorate it further. Alternatively, stick on gold stars.

6. Knot a loop of fine gold thread then, with a needle, thread the loop through several gold beads. Attach the loop on to the bauble with a pin.

WHAT YOU NEED

Polystyrene balls in various sizes

Paper serviettes or wrapping paper decorated with angels

Wallpaper paste

Paintbrush

Fuse wire or fine copper wire

Pins

Small feathers

Metallic gold paint

Gold beads in various sizes

Small gold stars

Sewing needle

Fine gold thread

Scissors

Baroque baubles

These baubles are textured with swirls of string and decorated with metallic paints.

1. Wind a length of string vertically around a polystyrene ball. Fix the string in place using pins. Rotate the ball 90° then repeat to divide the ball up into four equal segments. Now wind the string horizontally to divide the ball into eight segments.

2. Cut a small piece of string and lay it in one of the segments on the ball in a swirl or a loop. Fix in place with pins, then mirror the pattern in the facing segment. Repeat until you have filled up all the segments.

3. Mix up a small amount of wallpaper paste following the instructions on the packet. Brush it on to the string-covered ball.

4. Tear tissue paper into small pieces and stick them on to the ball. Once you have built up one layer, apply another coat of wallpaper paste, then continue papering until you have three layers in total. Leave to dry.

5. Paint the ball with metallic gold paint. Leave to dry and then sponge on metallic bronze and then copper paint. Leave to dry.

6. Thread pins with gold beads and stick them in to the ball to decorate it further. Use one of the pins to attach a hanging loop of gold thread on to the finished bauble.

WHAT YOU NEED

Polystyrene balls in various sizes

String

Pins

Wallpaper paste

White tissue paper

Scissors

Paintbrush

Metallic gold, copper and bronze paint

Sponge

Gold beads

Gold thread

Golden shapes and baubles

Simple materials can be used to create sophisticated effects.

Golden shapes

1. Trace the patterns on page 54 on to thin plywood or MDF.

2. Secure the wood in a clamp, and then cut out the shapes with a fret-saw or a jig-saw.

3. Bore a small hole in the top of each of the shapes.

4. Sandpaper all of the edges until smooth.

5. Paint the wooden shapes with gold paint. Leave to dry.

6. Create an antique effect by applying burnt umber paint to the shape using a rag.

7. Thread lengths of gold string through the holes to make hanging loops.

String baubles

1. Brush the top of a polystyrene ball or cone with glue.

2. Attach one end of the string to the top of the ball or cone using a pin. Arrange the string over the glue in a tight spiral. Press firmly down. Brush on a little more glue and continue to wind the string around the ball until it is covered. If you want to create pattern and texture, try alternating with different string.

3. Make a string loop. Paint the loop and the string-covered ball with two or three coats of gold paint. Leave to dry.

4. Attach the loop to the finished bauble with a pin.

WHAT YOU NEED

Golden shapes

Thin plywood or MDF
Tracing paper
Fret-saw or jig-saw
Clamp
Sandpaper
Gimlet/drill
Metallic gold paint
Burnt umber paint
Paintbrush
Rag
Gold string
Pencil

String baubles and cones

Polystyrene balls or cones in various sizes
String
Pins
Glue
Metallic gold paint
Paintbrush

Cardboard treasure

Corrugated cardboard is embellished with gold paint to make crowns, moons, hearts and stars.

Crowns

1. Coat a polystyrene ball with wallpaper paste (see page 11) and then cover it with pieces of absorbent paper to create a textured surface. Leave to dry.

2. Paint the ball with metallic bronze paint. When dry, sponge on gold paint.

3. Using a craft knife and a ruler, cut a strip of corrugated cardboard, about 25mm (1in) wide and long enough to encircle the ball, allowing for a 25mm (1in) overlap. Stick together the ends of the strip to form a ring.

4. Apply glue to the inside of the ring and then set the ball into the ring.

5. Cut out two thin strips of corrugated cardboard. Glue them on to the ball to divide it up into four equal sections. Trim the ends neatly.

6. Construct the arcs around the crown from strips of corrugated cardboard. Make sure the arcs are spaced evenly around the orb. Fix each end on to the centre of the orb and on to the ring of the crown using pins threaded with gold beads.

7. Decorate the ring of the crown with two narrow cardboard strips then glue a loop of gold thread on to the top of the orb.

Moons, hearts and stars

1. Trace the patterns on page 55 on to corrugated cardboard.

2. Cut out the stars using a craft knife and a ruler. Cut out the moons and hearts with a small pair of curved scissors.

3. Wind gold string around the shapes. Either knot the ends neatly or tie them in small bows.

4. Attach hanging loops of gold string.

WHAT YOU NEED

Crowns
Polystyrene balls in
  various sizes
Wallpaper paste
Absorbent paper
Paintbrush
Metallic bronze and gold
  paint
Sponge
Gold corrugated
  cardboard
Pencil and ruler
Scissors
Craft knife
Hot glue and glue gun
Pins
Gold beads
Gold thread

Moons , hearts and
  stars
Gold corrugated
  cardboard
Pencil and ruler
Tracing paper
Craft knife
Small curved scissors
Gold string

15

Stone-effect decorations

Bells, stars and moons are painted to look like stone and are decorated with gold glitter paint and coiled wire.

WHAT YOU NEED

For both decorations

Sand-coloured stone-
  effect paint
Paintbrush
Pencil and ruler
Craft knife
Hot glue and glue gun
Sewing needle and
  thread

Bells

Polystyrene bells and
  balls in various sizes
Gold glitter paint
Gold corrugated
  cardboard
Scissors
Gold string
Pins

Stars and moons

Natural-coloured and
  gold corrugated
  cardboard
Tracing paper
Small curved scissors
Coiled fuse wire

Bells

1. Paint a polystyrene bell and small ball with several coats of stone-effect paint.

2. Cut out a narrow strip of corrugated cardboard using a craft knife and a ruler. Wrap the strip around the bottom edge of the bell and fix in place with glue.

3. Decorate the bottom edge and the middle of the bell with gold string.

4. Paint over the bell with gold glitter paint.

5. Thread a needle with a double length of thread. Pierce through the ball with the needle and then through the top of the bell. Adjust the ball so that it hangs halfway down, then knot the thread to hold it in place. Leave both ends of the thread hanging from the top of the bell.

6. Make a hanging loop from a thin strip of cardboard. Attach the ends to the top of the bell with a pin. Tie the ends of the thread around the loop and then knot them.

Stars and Moons

1. Trace the star and moon patterns on page 55 on to natural-coloured and gold corrugated cardboard.

2. Cut out the stars using a craft knife and a ruler. Cut out the moons using a small pair of curved scissors.

3. Paint the stars and moons with two coats of stone-effect paint.

4. Glue the small stone-painted stars on to the large gold stars and vice versa.

5. Wrap the stars and moons with coiled fuse wire. Attach hanging loops of sewing thread.

Red and Green

The contrasting colours of red and green are traditionally associated with Christmas. The following chapter shows how effective these colours are and how you can make Christmas tree decorations from fabric, felt, modelling materials and corrugated cardboard.

Fabric baubles and garlands

Unique Christmas tree decorations can be made simply from festive fabric.

WHAT YOU NEED

Patchwork baubles

Polystyrene balls in
 various sizes
Festive material
Gold string
Red ribbon
Red and gold ribbon
 bows
Gold bells
Craft knife
Sharp knife or nail file
Felt-tip pen
Pins
Scissors
Glue

Plaited garlands

Festive material
Macramé yarn
Fine wire
Darning needle
Red ribbon
Red ribbon bows
Scissors
Glue

Patchwork baubles

1. Divide a polystyrene ball up into a minimum of four equal segments with a felt-tip pen.

2. Cut along the felt-tip lines with a craft knife to a depth of about 10mm (³/₈in).

3. Cut festive material into pieces slightly larger than each segment. Place a piece of material over one of the segments and push the edges into the grooves using the tip of a knife or a nailfile. Cut off any surplus material at the corners and hide the edges in the grooves. Continue until all the segments are covered.

4. Stick gold string over the grooves using a little glue.

5. Fix a hanging ribbon to the ball with a pin. Decorate with ribbon bows and a little bell.

Plaited garlands

1. Cut three 40 x 250mm (1¹/₂ x 10in) strips from the festive material and three 250mm (10in) lengths from the macramé yarn.

2. Brush the wrong side of each of the fabric strips with a generous amount of glue. Place each piece of macramé yarn on a long edge of a fabric strip then roll up the fabric loosely. Press the material firmly together then leave to dry.

3. Make a plait with the three fabric ropes. Hide the edges of the fabric ropes inside the plait.

4. Shape the plait into a circle. Overlap the ends slightly and then bind them tightly together with wire.

5. Thread a darning needle with ribbon and then push this through the garland to make a hanging loop.

6. Cover up the join in the plait with a ribbon bow.

Padded felt decorations

Felt is used to make a Father Christmas, and stars, apples, holly and stockings.

1. Trace the patterns on page 56 on to thin cardboard. Cut out the shapes to produce templates.

2. Place each template on a coloured felt of your choice, then draw round them with a felt-tip pen. Repeat so that you have two of all the shapes. Cut out the shapes.

3. Glue the decorative elements on to both pieces of the basic shape. Allow to dry.

4. Apply a thin strip of glue to the inside edge of one of the basic shapes, leaving a gap of approximately 20mm (³/₄in). Sandwich a hanging loop of gold string between both halves before sticking the shapes together. Leave the glue to dry.

5. Stuff wadding into the gap to pad out the decoration. When complete, stick together the open edges.

6. Clip the outside edge of the Father Christmas with pinking shears. For the other decorations, trim the edges with ordinary scissors.

7. Draw on the face of Father Christmas with a felt-tip pen. Glue on a little wadding to make the white trim of his hat and his beard.

WHAT YOU NEED

Red, dark red, green and white felt

Thin cardboard

Tracing paper

Pencil

Gold string

Wadding

Glue

Scissors

Pinking shears

Felt-tip pen

23

Modelled apples and stockings

*Papier mâché and air-drying clay are used to make
unusual stockings and apples.*

WHAT YOU NEED

Apples

Ready-mix papier
  mâché

Modelling stick

Cotton wool

Sandpaper

Red, green and brown
  paint

Satin finish clear
  varnish

Paintbrush

Gold string

Glue

Stockings

Air-drying clay

Thin cardboard

Tracing paper

Rolling pin

Water

Modelling stick

Drinking straw

Knife

Red, green and white
  paint

Satin finish clear
  varnish

Paintbrush

Gold string

Pencil

Scissors

Apples

1. Mix up a small amount of papier mâché following the instructions on the packet. Knead the pulp until malleable, then allow to stand for half an hour.

2. Apply the pulp to a ball of cotton wool, so as to keep the decoration light. Continue building up layers of pulp until you are happy with the size. Brush the ball of pulp with a little water then use your finger or a modelling stick to form the ball into the shape of an apple.

3. Make two small holes in the top of the apple using the end of a paintbrush.

4. Make a leaf and a stalk from small lumps of papier mâché. Draw in the veins of the leaf with the tip of a modelling stick. Stick the leaf and stalk into one of the holes in the top of the apple.

5. Leave to dry for a couple of days, then use sandpaper to smooth over the surface of the apple.

6. Paint the apple. When dry, apply a coat of varnish.

7. Make a hanging loop of gold string. Glue it into the second hole at the top of the apple.

Stockings

1. Place a lump of air-drying clay on aluminium foil. Roll it out to a thickness of about 5mm ($^1/_4$in).

2. Trace the stocking patterns on page 57 on to thin cardboard. Cut out the shapes to produce templates. Place the stocking template on the rolled-out clay. Hold a knife vertically to cut out the shape.

3. Roll out the rest of the clay to a thickness of about 3mm ($^1/_8$in). Cut out the leaves and the fur trim for the stockings as above.

4. Smooth all the edges of the cut-out shapes using a little water and your fingers.

5. Draw in the veins on the leaves using the tip of a modelling stick.

6. Brush the stocking with water then assemble all the pieces, pressing them firmly together to ensure that they stick.

7. Pierce the top of the fur trim with a straw.

8. Leave to dry on a flat surface, before painting and varnishing the stocking.

9. Thread a piece of gold string through the hole in the stocking, then tie it to make a hanging loop.

Cardboard shapes

These attractive decorations are made quickly and simply from coloured corrugated cardboard.

1. Trace the patterns on page 58 on to coloured corrugated cardboard. For each decoration, you will need mirror images of each of the shapes. Cut out all the shapes.

2. To make the parcels, sandwich a hanging loop of thread between the two main pieces before sticking them together with double-sided tape. Glue a bow to the front and back of the parcel.

3. To make the bells, thread a bead on to a short length of gold string, then sandwich this and a hanging loop of thread between two bell shapes. Stick the pieces together with double-sided tape. Thread a second bead on to the hanging thread. Glue a heart on to the front and back of the bell.

4. To make the candles, sandwich a long hanging loop of thread between the candle and large flame shapes, allowing a tiny gap between flame and candle. Stick together with double-sided tape. Glue the small flame shapes to the front and back of the large ones.

5. To make the Christmas trees, sandwich a hanging loop between the two pieces before sticking them together with double-sided tape. Stick on small gold stars to decorate.

WHAT YOU NEED

Red, gold and green
  corrugated cardboard
Tracing paper
Double-sided sticky tape
Gold string
Sewing thread
Red wooden beads
Small gold stars
Pencil
Scissors
Glue

Pastel Shades

If you want to move away from the traditional colours of gold, red and green, then try the decorations in this chapter – the delicate pastel shades will make a Christmas tree look good enough to eat.

Gift cones and bows

Treats can be hidden in these pretty gift cones, and the lace and satin bows look elegant on a tree.

WHAT YOU NEED

Gift cones

Pink cardboard
White paper doilies
Tracing paper
Pencil
Ruler
Craft knife
Scissors
Glue

Bows

White satin ribbon
White lace ribbon
Scissors
Fine wire
Pliers
Green florist's tape

Gift cones

1. Trace the pattern of the cone on page 59 on to coloured cardboard. Cut out the shape with a craft knife.

2. Make a crease along the dotted lines, using a ruler and the tip of a pair of scissors.

3. Cut four triangles from a doily; these should be approximately the same size as the four sections of the cone, only slightly shorter. Allow for a 10mm (¹/₂in) turnover at the base of each triangle.

4. Turn the cardboard over and position the doily triangles on top. Stick in place with glue. Fold down the edges at the base of each triangle and glue them to the cardboard.

5. Fold the cardboard along the dotted lines to form a cone shape. Dab the flap with glue and stick this to the inside of the cone.

6. Trace the strip on page 59 on to coloured cardboard. Cut it out, then glue it to the inside of the cone to make the handle.

Bows

1. Cut a 300mm (12in) length of satin ribbon. Fold the ends into the middle so that they overlap slightly, then secure with a piece of folded wire.

2. Make a small bow with a 230mm (10in) length of lace ribbon. Place it on top of the large satin bow. Fold the wire around the two bows to keep them in place.

3. Cover the wire binding with a short length of satin ribbon, secured at the back with a loose knot or stitched in place.

4. Bind the loose ends of wire with florist's tape – the covered wire can now be used as a clasp to attach the bow to the tree.

Coloured cardboard decorations

These musical notes and little parcels are simple to make but they look very effective.

Parcels

1. Trace the patterns for the parcel on page 59 on to coloured cardboard. Cut out all the shapes using a craft knife. For each parcel you will need one main box shape, and two lots of ribbons.

2. Glue the cardboard bows and ribbons on to the front and the back of the parcel.

3. Thread a needle then pull it through the top of the parcel's bow. Tie to form a hanging loop.

Musical Notes

1. Trace the musical note pattern on page 59 on to coloured cardboard.

2. Cut out the shape carefully using a craft knife.

3. Thread a needle then pull it through the top of the note. Tie to form a hanging loop.

WHAT YOU NEED

Pink, purple, blue and
  white cardboard

Tracing paper

Pencil

Ruler

Craft knife

Glue

Sewing needle and
  thread

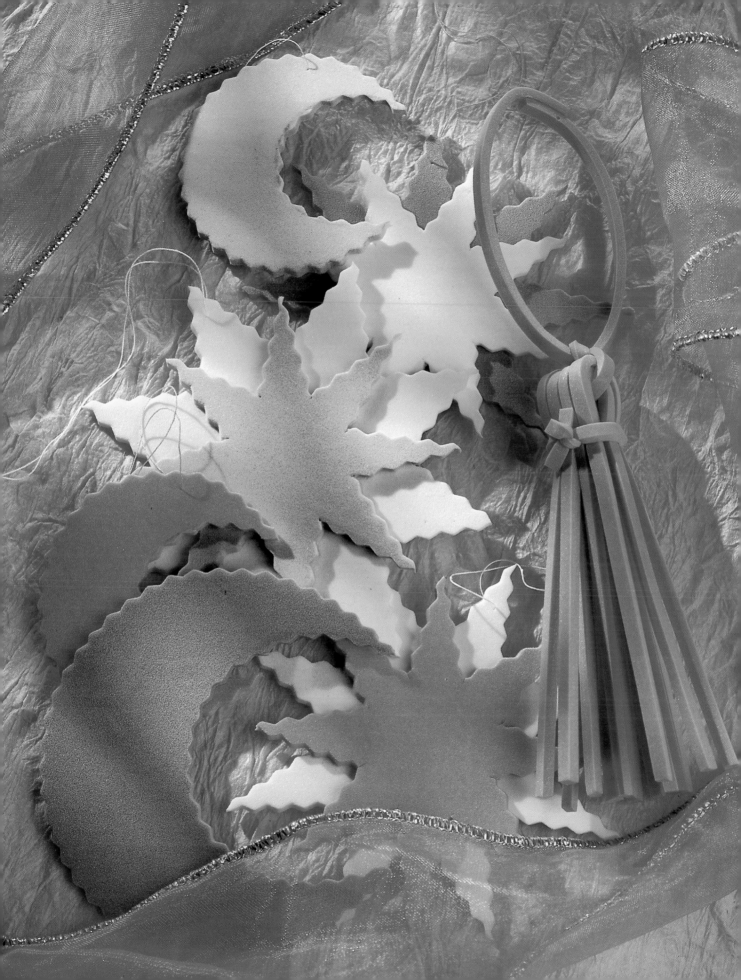

Foam decorations

These decorations were designed by a confectioner, which is why they look good enough to eat.

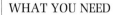

Tassels

1. Cut the foam into thin strips using a craft knife and a ruler – you will need one strip 300mm (12in) long; one strip 100mm (4in) long; and eight strips 200mm (8in) long.

2. Arrange the eight 200mm (8in) strips into a bundle then tie the 300mm (12in) strip around the middle in a double knot.

3. Fold the bundle in half then tie the 100mm (4in) strip in a double knot around the top of the bundle. Trim the ends off neatly.

4. Glue the ends of the hanging loop together, allowing for an overlap of approximately 10mm ($^1/_2$in).

Moons and stars

1. Trace the moon and star patterns on page 60 on to foam. The big and small stars should be traced on to different colours.

2. Cut out all the shapes with pinking shears.

3. Stick a small star on to a large one using a little glue.

4. Thread a needle and pierce the top of each decoration. Tie to form a hanging thread.

WHAT YOU NEED

Tassels

Pink fun foam

Pencil

Ruler

Craft knife

Scissors

Glue

Moons and Stars

White, pink, pale blue and lilac fun foam

Tracing paper

Soft pencil

Pinking shears

Glue

Sewing needle and thread

Miniature houses

These unusual little houses are made with cardboard and cellophane, allowing light to shine through the windows.

1. Trace the patterns for the houses on page 61 on to coloured cardboard.

2. Cut out the shapes of the houses, including the spaces for the doors and windows, using a craft knife.

3. Glue clear cellophane to the back of each house. You could use a coloured cellophane to produce a different effect.

3. Thread a needle then pierce it through the top of each house. Tie the thread to form hanging loops.

WHAT YOU NEED

Burgundy, mauve and
  beige cardboard

Tracing paper

Clear cellophane

Pencil

Craft knife

Glue

Sewing needle and
  thread

Natural Tones

If you want to get away from the glitzy colours traditionally associated with Christmas, then choose the following decorations to give your tree a more natural look. All the decorations shown are simple to make, and employ natural materials such as seeds, dried fruit and spices.

Hessian decorations

Natural fabric is combined with herbs and spices such as cinnamon, aniseed, rosemary and ginger to produce a range of unusual decorations.

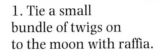

Preparation

1. Transfer the basic patterns on page 62 on to hessian (burlap); you will need two shapes for each decoration (see page 23). Cut out the shapes, leaving a small seam allowance. For the little bag, cut out a hessian (burlap) rectangle 100 x 250mm (4 x 10in).

2. Lay identical shapes on top of each other. Machine-sew the edges using a zig-zag stitch. Leave a gap of about 20mm (³/₄in). Stuff wadding into the gap, then sew it up. For the little bag, leave the top open, and then fill the bag up with wadding. Trim the edges of the hessian (burlap).

3. Glue a raffia hanging loop on to the top of each decoration.

Stars

1. Place a piece of ginger in the centre of the star. Wind a length of raffia over it to hold it in place. Knot the ends to make a hanging loop.

Christmas trees

1. Apply a zig-zag of glue to the Christmas tree, then scatter rosemary over it.

2. Trace the small tree, angel and heart patterns on page 62 on to cardboard. Cut them out then glue them on to the main tree.

Moons

1. Tie a small bundle of twigs on to the moon with raffia.

2. Glue a few aniseed stars on to the moon.

Hearts

1. Sew natural braid around the edge of the heart, and a tassel to the point.

2. Trace two of each of the smaller hearts in the pattern on page 62 on to handmade paper and corrugated cardboard. Glue on to both sides of the decoration. Glue rosemary on to one of the hearts.

Little bags

1. Tie the top of the bag with string. Wrap raffia around a bundle of cinnamon sticks. Decorate with a string bow then glue the bundle on to the bag.

2. Cut out a large star from corrugated cardboard and a small one from wide mesh ribbon (you can trace stars from the patterns on page 55 if you like). Stick the small star on to the large one. Decorate further by gluing on mixed herbs.

WHAT YOU NEED

Hessian (burlap)
Raffia
Wadding
Thin cardboard
Tracing paper
Natural-coloured corrugated cardboard
Handmade paper
String
Natural-coloured tassels
Natural-coloured braid
Dried rosemary
Ginger
Wide mesh ribbon
Dried mixed herbs
Cinnamon sticks
Aniseed stars
Small twigs
Sewing machine
Natural-coloured thread
Scissors
Hot glue and glue gun
Pencil

Fruit and spice decorations

These decorations have a festive perfume of citrus fruit, cloves and cinnamon.

Orange pendants

1. To make the orange pendants at the bottom of the picture opposite, wrap coiled fuse wire around a dried orange slice. Glue a raffia bow to the top of the orange slice. Decorate with an aniseed star or fuse wire coiled around cloves. Pull a length of raffia through the top of the pendant and tie to make a hanging loop.

2. To make the orange pendant in the middle of the picture opposite, wrap coiled fuse wire around a dried orange slice. Trace the little Christmas tree pattern on page 62 on to corrugated cardboard. Cut it out then pierce it with cloves. Stick the tree on to the middle of the orange slice and finish with a raffia hanging loop.

3. To make the orange pendant at the top of the picture opposite, apply glue to an orange slice and then scatter fruit tea on to it. Attach a bow made from string entwined with gold thread, then finish with a raffia hanging loop.

Spice chains

1. To make the cinnamon chain, plait three 600mm (24in) lengths of raffia and incorporate cinnamon sticks into the plait as you go. Tie the beginning and the end of the plait with a knot. Tie together several cinnamon plaits to form a big chain.

2. To make the aniseed chain, glue aniseed stars on to a length of string entwined with gold thread. Thread wooden beads on to a length of gold wire. Use as many wooden beads as you have used aniseed stars. Wind the gold wire around the string, positioning a wooden bead in the centre of each aniseed star as you go.

WHAT YOU NEED

For both decorations
String
Gold thread
Raffia
Hot glue and glue gun
Scissors

Orange pendants
Dried orange slices
Coiled fuse wire or fine
  copper wire
Cloves
Loose fruit tea
Aniseed stars
Natural-coloured
  corrugated cardboard

Spice chains
Cinnamon sticks
Aniseed stars
Small wooden beads
Gold wire

WHAT YOU NEED

For all the baubles

Polystyrene balls in
   various sizes
Skewers
PVA glue
Hot glue and glue gun
Scissors
Natural-coloured ribbon
Gold string

Fruit tea baubles

String
Brown sugar crystals
Loose fruit tea

Buckwheat baubles

Buckwheat
Gold string
Gold fir cones

Mustard seed baubles

Mustard seeds
Cinnamon sticks
Ginger
Gold string

Rosemary baubles

Dried rosemary
Green string
Dried twigs
Small wooden beads

Flax seed baubles

Flax seeds
Gold string
Dried fruit

Seed, herb and spice baubles

A kitchen cupboard and a spice rack are the inspiration for this selection of baubles.

1. Stick a skewer into a polystyrene ball then cover the ball with PVA glue.

2. Place the seed, herb or spice of your choice into a shallow dish, and then roll the glue-covered ball into the dish to coat it.

3. Allow the glue to dry thoroughly. Add more glue and seeds, herbs or spices to cover the ball as necessary.

4. Glue bows made out of natural-coloured ribbon on to the bauble to decorate it further.

5. Glue a hanging loop of gold string on to the top of the bauble.

6. Finally, decorate the bow with the materials specified in the list opposite.

Corrugated cardboard decorations

Corrugated cardboard is decorated with natural materials such as wood, leather, string, fabric and seeds.

Preparation

1. Trace the basic patterns on page 63 on to corrugated cardboard. You will need mirror images of each shape for each decoration. Cut out the shapes using a craft knife.

2. For each decoration (except the pendant), sandwich a cream leather cord hanging loop between two pieces before sticking them together.

Hearts

1. Glue braided cord around the cardboard heart.

2. Working from the patterns on page 63, cut out a small heart from dark brown cardboard and a large one from hessian (burlap). Glue sesame seeds around the edge of the cardboard heart and a wooden dome to the front of the hessian (burlap) heart. Attach them to the front and back of the main heart.

Christmas trees

1. Glue string around the edge of the tree. Cut out small stars from dark brown cardboard (see pattern on page 63) then glue them to the back and front of the tree.

2. Stick small pieces of fir cone to the front of the tree.

Shooting stars

1. Glue dark brown leather cord and a line of sesame seeds around the edge of the star.

2. Pierce the middle of the star twice with the tip of a pencil. Thread through a length of leather cord. Thread wooden beads on to the cord then knot the ends. Glue a raffia bow to the centre of the star.

Pendants

1. Wind raffia around the cardboard circle. Tie the ends with a bow. Thread a raffia hanging loop through the back of the bow.

2. Glue dark brown leather cord around the edge of the pendant and tie the top of it in a bow. Thread wooden beads on to the ends of the cord and finish with a knot.

Stars

1. Glue a plait of raffia around the edge of the star and its lower point.

2. Thread a few short lengths of raffia with wooden bells and stick them to the top of the star.

3. Thread a wooden bead over the leather hanging loop, then attach pieces of fir cone to the front and back of the top of the star.

WHAT YOU NEED

Natural-coloured and dark brown corrugated cardboard

Tracing paper

Raffia

Wooden beads in various sizes

String

Cream and dark brown leather cord

Braided cord

Small wooden domes

Fir cones

Small wooden bells

Hessian (burlap)

Sesame seeds

Pencil

Craft knife

Hot glue and glue gun

Muslin and net decorations

Natural netting is lined with muslin and decorated with natural materials.

Preparation

1. Transfer the basic patterns on page 62 on to wide mesh hessian (burlap) and muslin; you will need two shapes from each fabric for each decoration (see page 23). Cut out the shapes, leaving a small seam allowance. For the little bag, cut out a hessian (burlap) rectangle 100 x 250mm (4 x 10in).

2. Lay identical shapes on top of each other, with the two pieces of muslin sandwiched on the inside. Machine-sew the edges together using a zig-zag stitch. Leave a gap of about 20mm ($^3/_4$in). Stuff wadding into the gap, then sew it up. For the little bag, leave the top open, and then fill the bag up with wadding. Trim the edges of the hessian (burlap).

Moons

1. Cut out two small hessian (burlap) rectangles. Place them on the front and back of the moon and wrap raffia around them. Glue raffia bows on top of them.

2. Thread a wooden bead on to a length of string. Thread the string through the hessian (burlap) moon and tie to make a hanging loop.

Bells

1. Make a long, loose loop of raffia around the length of the bell. Thread a wooden bead through the bottom of the raffia loop, and bind the top with string bows.

Stars

1. Wrap string around the points of the star, then thread the ends through the hessian (burlap) to make a hanging loop. Thread a wooden bead through the loop and attach a tassel to the end.

Hearts

1. Apply a diagonal line of glue to the heart. Sprinkle fruit tea on top.

2. Make a bow and a hanging loop from string and glue to the top of the heart.

Little bags

1. Tie the top of the bag with lengths of raffia and string.

2. Thread slices of dried apple through the ends of the raffia and secure with a knot.

WHAT YOU NEED

Muslin

Wide mesh hessian (burlap)

Hessian (burlap)

Thin cardboard

Tracing paper

String

Raffia

Wooden beads 16mm ($^5/_8$in) in diameter

Natural-coloured tassels

Dried apple slices

Loose fruit tea

Wadding

Scissors

Sewing machine

Natural-coloured sewing thread

Hot glue and glue gun

Pencil

Rustic tassels and bundles

Raffia and dried twigs are used to make Christmas tassels and bundles.

WHAT YOU NEED

For both decorations
Raffia
Wide mesh hessian
  (burlap)
Hot glue and glue gun
Scissors

Raffia tassels
Wooden beads, 35 and
  10mm (1³/₈ and ¹/₂in)
  in diameter
Natural-coloured and
  green string
Dried rosemary
Aniseed stars

Twig Bundles
Dried twigs
String
Gold thread
Gold wire
Miniature parcels

Raffia tassels

1. Cut the raffia into 300mm (12in) lengths. Gather a bundle of the cut raffia, then fold it in half.

2. To make the middle tassel, glue the folded end of the raffia bundle into the hole of a large wooden bead. Place a square of wide mesh hessian (burlap) over the wooden bead and bind it underneath with string. Stick the ends of the string down with glue. Thread two small wooden beads on to a hanging loop of raffia. Glue the ends of the loop into the hole in the top of the large wooden bead.

3. To make the other two tassels, coat two large wooden beads with glue. Dip one of the beads in rosemary, and spiral string around the other one. Glue a raffia bundle into each bead as described above. Attach a hanging loop of raffia to each bead. Thread a small wooden bead on to the hanging loop on the string-covered decoration and stick a raffia bow and aniseed star underneath the main bead. Bind the rosemary tassel with green string above and below the wooden bead.

Bundles of twigs

1. Break dried twigs roughly into 180mm (7in) lengths. Gather them into small bundles.

2. To make the bundle in the bottom left of the picture, bind the twigs with string. Leave the ends of the string hanging down, and wind gold thread around them before tying with a knot. Make a hanging loop of string encircled with gold wire. Attach it to the middle of the bundle and then decorate with a raffia bow.

3. To make the bundle in the bottom right of the picture, bind the twigs with wide mesh hessian (burlap) and then with a plait of raffia. Glue a miniature parcel to the middle of the bundle. Thread a hanging loop of raffia through the string on the parcel.

4. To make the bundle in the top left of the picture, bind the twigs with string and raffia, and finish with a bow. Attach a hanging loop of raffia.

Terracotta decorations

Angels, stars, hearts, clubs and spades are made in earthy terracotta tones.

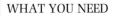

Angels

1. Place a ball of air-drying clay on to aluminium foil then roll it out to a thickness of about 5mm (^{1}/$_4$in).

2. Trace the angel patterns on page 57 on to thin cardboard then cut out the shapes to make templates. Place the body template on the clay and cut around it with a knife.

3. Wrap the shape into a cone, overlapping the short edges. Brush the cone with a little water, then smooth over the join and the inside of the cone with your finger to make a more rounded shape.

4. Pierce a hole horizontally either side of the top of the cone with a drinking straw.

5. Shape a ball for the head, brush it with a little water and attach it to the body. Make the mouth using a straw and draw in the eyes and nostrils with a modelling stick. Feed clay through a garlic press to make the hair. Dampen the head and then attach the hair.

6. Roll out a ball of clay to a thickness of about 3mm (^{1}/$_8$in). Cut out the wings, heart and star. Brush them with a little water and attach them to the body.

7. Make rolls of clay for the arms, and small balls for the hands. Shape the ends of the sleeves with a modelling stick, then brush them with water and attach the hands. Pierce a hole in the top of each arm.

6. Leave the pieces to dry, then paint and varnish them.

7. Thread string through the holes in the body and arms then knot to form a hanging loop.

Hearts, stars, clubs and spades

1. Place a ball of air-drying clay on aluminium foil then roll it out to a thickness of about 3mm (^{1}/$_8$in). Lay a piece of towelling over the clay then roll over it with a rolling pin to create a textured surface.

2. Trace the patterns on page 57 on to thin cardboard and cut out the shapes to make templates. Place the templates on top of the clay and cut round them with a knife.

2. Pierce a hole at the top of each decoration then leave all the pieces to dry on a flat surface.

3. Varnish the decorations. When dry, thread green cord through the holes and make hanging loops.

WHAT YOU NEED

For both the models
Red air-drying clay
Thin cardboard
Tracing paper
Pencil
Scissors
Rolling pin
Aluminium foil
Water
Small knife
Drinking straw
Clear matt varnish
Paint brush

Angels
Modelling stick
Garlic press
Brown, green and gold paint
String

Hearts, stars, clubs and spades
Towelling
Green cord

Patterns
(Pages 12/13)

(Pages 22/23)

(Pages 26/27)

58

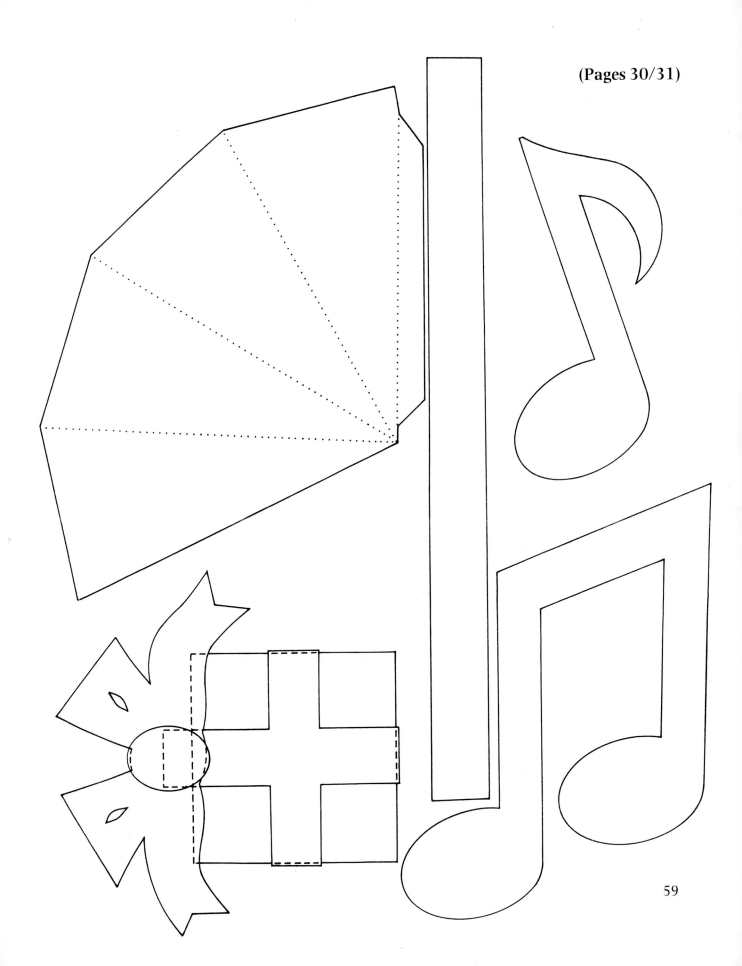

(Pages 34/35)

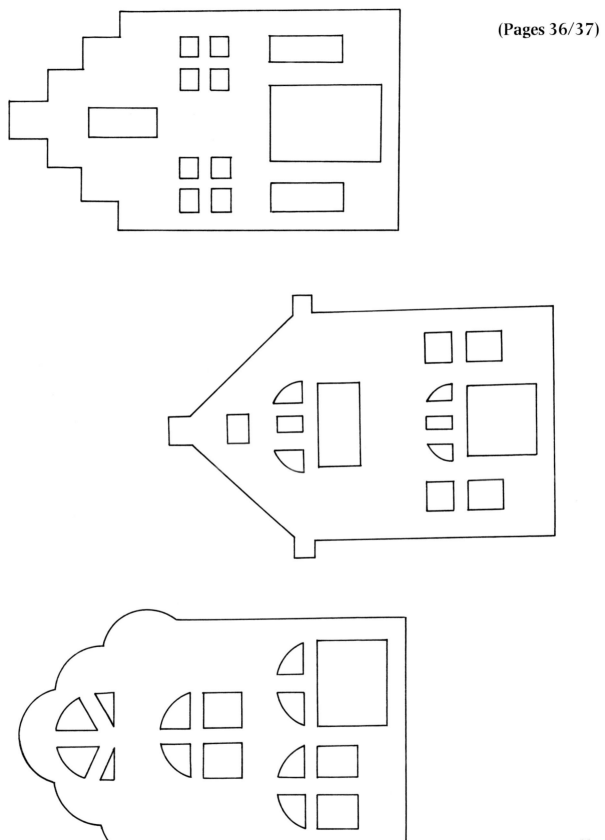

Index